SURROUNDED BY IDIOTS

How Ineffective Communication Causes Chaos

B. T. Goodwin

© Copyright 2020 - All rights reserved.

The content contained within this book may not be reproduced, duplicated or transmitted without direct written permission from the author or the publisher.

Under no circumstances will any blame or legal responsibility be held against the publisher, or author, for any damages, reparation, or monetary loss due to the information contained within this book, either directly or indirectly.

Legal Notice:

This book is copyright protected. It is only for personal use. You cannot amend, distribute, sell, use, quote or paraphrase any part, or the content within this book, without the consent of the author or publisher.

Disclaimer Notice:

Please note the information contained within this document is for educational and entertainment purposes only. All effort has been executed to present accurate, up to date, reliable, complete information. No warranties of any kind are declared or implied. Readers acknowledge that the author is not engaged in the rendering of legal, financial, medical or professional advice. The content within this book has been derived from various sources. Please consult a licensed professional before attempting any techniques outlined in this book.

By reading this document, the reader agrees that under no circumstances is the author responsible for any losses, direct or indirect, that are incurred as a result of the use of the information contained within this document, including, but not limited to, errors, omissions, or inaccuracies.

Table of Contents

Table of Contents	4
Introduction	7
Chapter 1: Signs You May Be the Problem	11
The Five Stages of Realization	12
Denial	12
Anger	12
Bargaining	12
Depression	13
Acceptance	13
The Dawning of Self-Awareness	14
Ineffective Communication Skills	14
The "You" Factor	14
Invalidating a Person's Feelings	15
Personalizing the Issue Instead of Focusing on the Problem	16
Sarcasm	16
Passive-Aggressiveness	17
Concentrating on the Negatives	17
Chapter 2: How to Realize You May Be the Issue	21
Know the Signs	22
The Truth Hurts	23
The Aftermath of Ineffective Communication	24
Side Effects of Ineffective Communication	24
Chapter 3: Overcoming Ineffective Communication	29
Chapter 4: Effective Communication Tactics for the Workplace	35
Good Communication in the Workplace	36
Tips and Tactics for Better Communication in the Workplace	37
Where to Start Communicating Effectively at Work	41

Chapter 5: Effective Communication Tactics for Relationships	45
Effectively Communicating Your Way Through Relationships	46
Where to Start Communicating Effectively in a Relationship	50
Chapter 6: The Art of Communicating With Children, Tweens, and Teens	55
Where to Start Communicating Effectively With Children	59
Chapter 7: Effective Communication Tactics for Everyday Life	67
Where to Start Effectively Communicating in Everyday Life	70
Chapter 8: Characteristics of an Effective Communicator	75
Body Language	80
Chapter 9: Building Effective Communication Bridges	85
The Difference Between a Talker and a Communicator	88
Quick Simple Exercises to Practice Effective Communication	89
Chapter 10: Sarcasm and Passive-Aggressiveness	93
Sarcasm	94
Passive-Aggression	95
Conclusion	99
References	103

Introduction

Are you that person who others must warn people about before they introduce you? Do you often feel as if you are swimming in a sea filled with incompetent idiots that run around like headless chickens? If people voice their opinions, it is nothing but clucking to you, anyway!

You may even feel you have the fittest eyeballs around as all you seem to do is roll them at the sheer idiocy of people around you. You probably feel you must be the only intelligent being on this earth. While you may think you know or have all the answers, there is also the possibility that you did not understand the situation.

While there are different levels of intelligence, even the most intelligent people do not know everything. Even a genius can learn something from someone not at their level of intelligence. After all, there is always more than one way to look at something, and no two people ever see something the same. For instance, two people can look at the same painting but see it in a different light.

If you took a step back for a minute and tried to see the situation through another's eyes, you may see that perhaps it is you who is the idiot and not them. It does not matter if you are an expert in your field, have all the answers, or are the world's most intelligent person. If you do not know how to effectively communicate with others, it is not them who is at fault, but you.

If you purchased this book on your own, then it shows your willingness to learn more about yourself and how to effectively communicate with others. If someone gave you this book as a gift, that is a passive-aggressive attempt to get you to recognize your communication fails.

"Surrounded by Idiots: How Ineffective Communication Causes Chaos" is filled with advice and tactics to help you improve your communication skills in your everyday life.

This should take you no more than 2-3 days to finish. I did this for good reason, advice should be short and concise. The faster you ingest this information, the faster you can make a change in your life and others around you.

Chapter 1
Signs You May Be the Problem

Realizing you represent the problem is never a pleasant thing to come to terms with. In fact, it is almost like experiencing the five stages of grief when the reality hits you. For the sake of this book, these stages will be referred to as "The Five Stages of Realization" because when the truth dawns on you, it is like experiencing the five stages of grief.

The Five Stages of Realization

Once you realize you are the idiot, it can be a rather hard pill to swallow. No one enjoys facing the fact that they are the problem and have been all along. It is what makes self-doubt creep in, a concept that was probably never a problem for you before. In fact, most people who are here reading this book were probably overly confident of themselves.

You will experience the following stages of realization before you come to terms with your own imperfections.

Denial
First, you will deny it, because how could it be you? It is not your fault other people are complete morons! Why should you take the blame for their incompetence?

Does that sound familiar to you? It is what your first reaction to realizing **you** were the one in the wrong will more than likely be. Right now, you are probably denying; denying it just to prove this theory wrong! Don't worry; it is a normal reaction to having a finger pointing at you for a change.

Anger
Once the denial ebbs a bit, the anger will hit you. This stage will make you angry at the world, or at least, you will think you are angry at the world. In fact, you are angry at yourself, only you are still a little in denial, so the world will still be full of idiots.

Bargaining
Once the anger subsides and you rationalize your thoughts or feelings, the bargaining starts. You will wonder what you could have done differently to begin with. You will try to remember when

your life went so horribly wrong you became the idiot that you yourself cannot tolerate. Suddenly that "if only" state of mind sets in and you try to figure out what you could have or should have done differently.

Depression
Depression will hit in a few forms. First, you will feel like the worst person on earth. You will feel like no one even likes you, let alone tolerates or loves you. You will even doubt those who are your loved ones. The second form of depression will have you withdrawing into yourself as you no longer feel in control. You have suddenly realized you are not the person you thought you were or the golden boy/girl you were sure people saw you as. This is the "feeling sorry for yourself" stage. Now the world is full of people who may not be as intelligent as you, but they are by far better people than you are.

Acceptance
The first three to four stages of acceptance may become an endless loop as you recycle through them repeatedly. It is not easy to change habits or a lifetime of being yourself instantly. You may as well be grieving a loss because it is one and because you realize you lost something along the way. The void left by the loss was filled by something else for which you never meant to fill it. Acceptance comes once you have completely accepted the fact that somewhere along the way you got lost. Instead of taking the time to figure it out, you covered it up with sarcasm, making impossible demands, and more than likely being demeaning to others. Acceptance comes when you take the initiative to change your ways, learn how to communicate, and make an honest effort to be a pleasant person share oxygen with. It usually doesn't hurt to start making amends with those you have alienated either. Now that you have accepted this fact, stop reading and go to your nearest mirror and say out loud:

"YOU ARE A BAD COMMUNICATOR, BUT IT IS OK. <u>WE WILL WORK ON THIS</u>"

The Dawning of Self-Awareness
When you first read this book, you are probably doing so with gritted teeth. Most people would rather opt to wrestle a bear than the truth about themselves. So, most people live their lives in denial. Well, at least those who are not like you but are willing to at least do some research or give a few tactics a go. That is why the five stages of realization are one of the first things you read about in this book. It is to prepare you for what is coming as you read on and recognize some of your destructive communication habits. It will get even worse when you read how your lack of skills has affected others. The more you read, the more you will come to realize you may not be the communicator you think you are. Before you have finished this chapter, you will have become self-aware of your actions and responses to others around you. If you are willing to put in the work and think before you rush in guns blazing, you will notice things are changing around you. People may ask you to go to lunch, someone may swap a day off with you, and overall, you may notice the pleasantries of working and relating with others.

Ineffective Communication Skills
Before you walk down the path of the five stages of realization, you first need to know how to recognize the signs you may be a terrible communicator.

The first stage of the five stages of realization is denial. The following section highlights how to recognize you may represent the problem. Without proper communication skills, you may just be the one responsible for causing all the chaos around you and raising your stress levels.

The following points represent signs of poor communication skills:

The "You" Factor
The "you" factor is usually used along with a directive that can pass as an order or come across as being a negative judgment of someone. The "you" factor used with a directive is bound to get a person's defenses up. It can elicit arguments or no response at all. It mostly ends with lots of bad vibes hanging in the air between you and the person or people in question.

Some examples of the "**you**" factor used with a negative directive are:

- **You** people are just not getting it.
- **You** will never be good enough.
- **You** are going to fail if you do not listen.
- **You** must see things from my point of view.
- **You** had better get this done correctly.

If you use one or more of these factors or directives, you need to think to yourself how you feel when they are used on you.

No one likes to be judged and, to be fair, no one has a right to judge another. The "you" factor used with a negative directive makes a person feel like they have been tried, judged, and sentenced. So, if you are not getting the response you were hoping for using statements as mentioned above, you need to rethink the way you use the "you" factor. Not all uses of the "you" factor are bad, and it can be used amicably or positively. To use the "you" factor more positively, you could try saying,

"You didn't get it this time, but there is always a next time."

Invalidating a Person's Feelings
Poor communicators are insensitive to how the other person is feeling, or they blatantly disregard them. Some examples of disregarding, demeaning, belittling, or negatively judging a person's feelings are:

- "I do not care how you are feeling; this is all your fault."
- "Stop overreacting; no one cares if you are angry or upset."
- "You have no cause to be so happy about getting a B."
- "I find your complaints are unfounded."
- "No one wants to know about your silly concerns."
- "Why are you crying? Your tears will not fix this."

Some poor communicators may even use a person's emotions against them to make them feel even worse. They usually like to mix in the "you" factor to bring their point home. Some examples of using a person's emotions against them are:

- "Do you think you are feeling bad now? Just you wait and see how you feel if things do not improve."
- "Do you think feeling a little emotional over the issue will change anything?"
- "No one cares about your silly hurt feelings; suck it up and move on."

Note that poor communicators do not acknowledge or realize the feelings of others. They are just unequipped to handle them.

Personalizing the Issue Instead of Focusing on the Problem

Everyone makes mistakes or messes up; it is part of life. Poor communicators are quick to focus in and make a situation personal rather than focusing on the problem or situation. There are many elements to a problem or situation. Human error can cause problems or bring about a critical situation. But it is best to take a step back and concentrate on the problem, not attack the person deemed responsible for it. Nothing is more counterproductive than exploding at or berating the person thought to have caused the problem. It will not make the situation or problem go away.

Some examples of personalizing an issue are:

- "You are such a slob; you never clean up anything."
- "How can you be so stupid?"
- "You are a poor listener."

Poor communicators will yell around a situation, leaving matters, issues, and problems unresolved or poorly managed. This can lead to a hostile response which leads to a hostile environment.

Sarcasm

There is a time and place for a witty comment. Although you may think you are being smart, you are not; you are using sarcasm as a form of bullying. Bullies love to belittle their prey; using sarcasm to get a point across is no different.

Examples of using sarcasm include:

- "I know snails that would work faster than you."
- "You have fewer brains than a jellyfish."
- "Your plans are about as useful as a leaky boat in the middle of an ocean."

Sometimes, sarcasm is fine and can give a person a good giggle or make them think about something when used intelligently. But it can also belittle, demean, and hurt someone when aimed directly at them. As with everything in life, there is a time and place for things. Sometimes a person does not mind people laughing with them, but no one likes to be laughed at—that is just ignorant and cruel.

Passive-Aggressiveness
Passive-aggressiveness and sarcasm can be confused as the same thing. But sarcasm is a more aggressive form of verbal abuse or ridicule. It is directly aimed at the target of the sarcasm where both parties are aware of its intention to harm. Passive-aggressiveness is a more subtle form of hurting someone's feelings or making them feel small without direct aggression.

An example would be to hand someone this book and tell them they need to read it. The title alone is enough to trigger a negative reaction from the receiver.

Concentrating on the Negatives
There is a name for people who shoot down an idea before they have thought it through. We know these people as the "no man/woman" because they can only see the potential holes or negatives to anything.

By only choosing to see a negative side to anything makes a person come across as arrogant, unfeeling, and self-serving. Your plan is not the only one out there and someone may have a better one. It does not mean yours is not up to par, but maybe a fresh perspective can enhance your idea, or your idea could patch up the holes to the idea you just shot down.

Granted, some ideas may not be the best ones, but an excellent communicator knows to at least listen and how to ease in a better solution.

CHAPTER 2
How to Realize You May Be the Issue

Coming to terms with the fact that you may be the issue and not those around you is a process. The very first step in this process is to reflect on a day in the past week you felt the most frustrated or irritated with co-workers or people around you.

Know the Signs
It is time to do a bit of reflecting as you read through this chapter. If you can relate to one or more of the following scenarios, then you may have a communication problem. But do not despair; there is still hope for you, especially if you are willing to try and change how you communicate. By reading this book, you have already taken the first steps to improve your people skills. It is important to put your ego aside and be honest with yourself. There is no one else between these pages right now, as this is between you and this book.

Some signs you may be the problem include the following scenarios:

You Always Have All the Answers
You often feel you are the only one in the room who has all the answers. Everyone else's answers just don't measure up to the situation, and you feel you are the only one keeping things going.

You Feel You Are Not Getting Through to People
You feel as if no one quite gets what you are trying to convey. Their blank stares and stammering when asked direct questions suggest you lost their attention during the conversation. It could also be a case of you not getting your message through clearly enough or you had the wrong audience for the topic.

You Notice People Don't Ask You Questions
People are hesitant to ask you questions or for help. They may just avoid asking you altogether.

You Get a Lot of Passive Aggressive Attention
Does your inbox get filled with passive-aggressive emails, or you find that you are the target of this attention? For instance, your boss may suggest various people's skills seminars, communication courses, and so on.

You Multitask Instead of Giving Your Full Attention
Instead of taking the time to stop and give a conversation your full attention, you continue working, listening with half an ear. For good measure, you may give the speaker a few glances or offer a few words.

You Are Condescending
You always must be the one with all the ideas and shoot other people's ideas down. This makes you come across as if you are better than them and may even feel you are, especially as you feel you are surrounded by idiots. There is a fine line between cocky and confident; these can easily be misconstrued depending on how you are received.

You Interrupt a Lot
One thing no one likes is to be interrupted when they are trying to talk. Most ineffective communicators think they are contributing by their constant interruptions or finishing a person's sentences.

You Have an Experience for Nearly Everything
Everything someone else can do, you can probably do better. Everything someone else has done or experienced, you have experienced something similar or can better it.

The Truth Hurts
Once you have finished reading this book, come back to this chapter. Then no matter how hard it is to face the facts about your people skills, add to the list of scenarios above. Do so honestly by adding scenarios you feel made you a terrible communicator. Add these to the list, so you know what you need to work on or watch out for as you turn your skillset around.

It is important to keep in mind that no one else must see your list either. This is about you, admitting you have a problem and showing your willingness to do something about it. It is personal to you and of benefit to those who know you, work with you, and love you. It is up to you who you want to share your journey with. But those who love you will also provide you with the support you may need to break old habits and forge fresh ones.

The Aftermath of Ineffective Communication
Ineffective communication not only causes chaos in business or a person's everyday life, but it can also cause lots of emotional, if not physical, damage. In a work environment, it can lead to poor employee morale, a lack of engagement, and cause an unproductive environment.

In a person's personal or everyday life, it can lead to unnecessary conflict and tensions and create an unstable/unhappy environment. It can cause dysfunction in family units, leading to a very toxic environment that rarely ends well for anyone involved. In a work environment, it can lead to poor employee morale, a lack of engagement, and cause a hostile and unproductive environment. The ripple effect can take place since there are people out there that do not understand a work/life balance. Things that happen at work can trickle into home and vice versa.

Side Effects of Ineffective Communication
For the person or people on the receiving end of the communication, it can cause the following feelings or situations:

Uncertainty
Not communicating effectively can lead to lots of uncertainty in both the workplace and a person's personal life. Not wanting to disappoint, let down, or face the wrath of their peer(s) makes a person second guess themselves. They feel like they have to walk around on eggshells and are too afraid to approach the person to ask for help. **Bad communicators come across as unapproachable and not open for discussion.**

Uncertainty in the workplace can cause lots of problems as communication breaks down and employees would rather try covering things up than admit they have a problem. Not through a lack of trying on the employees' part, but out of fear of the consequences. If employees feel they cannot communicate with their supervisor or manager, then it will lead to a lack of knowledge and lots of productivity issues.

In a relationship, uncertainty causes issues of mistrust, misunderstanding, and a misinterpretation of situations. Any kind of breakdown such as these previously mentioned causes dysfunction and ultimately a breakup.

Morale Issues
In the workplace, keeping up good employee morale is important. Unhappy employees make for an unhappy workplace that can lead to a company's downfall or high staff turnover.

When you are constantly knocking at a person's self-esteem and nothing they do seems correct, they will rebel or withdraw. Rebelling means a huge office grapevine, staff that will not take your direction well, or may go right over your head.

The staff that withdraws will have low self-esteem that will lead to problems with them not producing top quality work, possibly starting to miss working days, or leaving. It can also lead to negative attitudes and the drumming up the support of other staff members.

In a person's personal life, it can lead to family breakups, tragedies, as well as rebellion. Your kids are in a stage of their lives where you are supposed to protect them and build them up. Ineffective communication can be detrimental to this and knock them down. This can lead to kids running away from home, bullying other kids, withdrawing from you, or worse.

In a relationship, it can cause the person to seek the comfort and attention they crave elsewhere. No one wants to be constantly attacked or made to feel nothing they can do pleases or is right. It has a tremendous impact on a person's morale being the constant target of an ineffective communicator who thinks everyone around them is an idiot.

Broken Relationships
Broken relationships can be work relationships, friendships, and family relationships. If you mistreat a person, it breaks them down mentally, emotionally, and physically. Eventually, they will no longer try communicating with you and either lash out at you or just cut all ties to you.

Not communicating correctly causes many problems between people as misunderstandings arise. This is closely followed by all those negative emotions such as anger, frustration, irritation, and mistrust.

Chapter 3
Overcoming Ineffective Communication

You may have been skimming through the first few chapters of this book. But if you are serious about wanting to improve on your communication skills, you need to pay close attention from this chapter onwards.

It is natural to be feeling a little put-out and have your defenses up right about now. You are also probably still stuck in the denial, anger, and bargaining loop of the stages of realization. Don't back down now; push forward. At least get to the end of the book!

By reading until the end of the book, you will have overcome the first hurdle of overcoming ineffective communication. You have managed to put aside your ego and pride to improve your people skills. This shows you are driven to better yourself!

Now that you have an inkling of what terrible communication is, you can change your awful habits. The following tactics can help you take the first steps to effectively communicating with others:

Getting Over Yourself
The first step is getting rid of or at least putting aside your ego and pride to admit fault. **<u>Get over yourself.</u>** So, you may not be the world's best communicator at the moment, and you have ruffled more than a few feathers. Yes, it matters that you have not been very nice to some people. It is not as if you cannot mend those bridges. It is not as if you cannot mend those bridges. Most relationships are salvageable, you just have to make a concerted effort to re-build a bilateral level of trust.

Before you go trying to mend bridges and change, you need to know how. As a person with these habits now deeply ingrained in you, your first thought was probably to rush off and fix the problem now! **STOP!** Rash decisions and lack of thinking things through is part of the problem. You have a little way to go yet before you get to the part of the mending bridges. Make sure you are paying attention to the small things along this journey.

Bad Habits to Be Aware Of
Now that you have more self-awareness, you will be more conscious of how you communicate. You feel more aware of how people see you. At first, this can be soul-crushing, especially when you realize that this is how you have always been seen.

Rushing In
Before you go rushing in with the accusations or want to butt in on a conversation or jump to conclusions, take a deep breath and don't do it.

STOP! THINK! LISTEN! THINK AGAIN!

Rushing in will be the hardest of the unwelcome habits to break. You think you are helping or saving the day in your way, but you are not. You need to take a more in-depth look and see the situation from a few angles before giving your two cents. Always observe and think from multiple perspectives. There are ways to frame and prime your mind to speak prior to actually doing so.

Things may not have been done to your specifications, but maybe there is an excellent reason for this. Listen, but with both ears and brain in gear, to the explanation. Then give it a little while to sink in before proceeding further.

At least give the explanation some thought and see it from the other person's perspective. If you take the time and mull over the problem before accusing or berating the person in question, you are more likely to get the truth. You will also get the problem solved a lot quicker and in a more amicable way.

You will be a lot more approachable to others, making yourself more open to them; ask your questions if they do not understand anything or need clarification. If you make yourself more approachable, you may not run into too many issues or problems.

Angry or Emotional Outbursts
If you are angry, apply the brakes immediately and cool yourself down. If you are in a meeting or a room with the source of your anger, excuse yourself and go calm down.

DETACH! CALM DOWN! THINK!

Anger is a nasty opponent in any situation. Before you know it, it has turned your tongue into a razor-sharp blade driven by a fiery brain. Words once spoken cannot be unspoken, and anger throws the most damaging words out there.

Anger also alienates you as no one wants to deal with a hothead. Your anger may be justified, to you anyway, but an effective communicator knows how to keep it in check. There is a time and place for everything. This is especially true for anger as it can damage both personal and working relationships.

Emotional outbursts should be kept in check. If you are upset or emotional, it is best not to make decisions or try to work anything out. This is easier said than done as irritation, frustration, and annoyance are also emotions. Keeping emotions in check does not always work out as they can overpower a person in a split second.

Until you have learned to master yours, it is best to DETACH! CALM DOWN! THINK. Another alternative would be to just walk away until you feel you can tackle the situation with a level head.

Think
Always think before you explain anything. Gage your audience and adjust your explanation accordingly. Once you learn to control your body language, it is easy to pick up on others.
In the workplace, go over past projects or similar situations and build your scenario around those. Going over similar situations will help you better know your audience, their strengths, and weaknesses and how to engage with them.

In relationships, it is always best to be sure you have listened and understood before you proceed. When you do proceed, try to do so with diplomacy and let the other person feel like you have considered their side of the story.

Pick the Time
Pick the right time and place to approach. If someone needs to be taken down a peg or two, it does not have to be done publicly; that accomplishes nothing. It just embarrasses the person and makes the situation much worse than it has to be.

If you want to pitch something, then the correct timing could mean the difference between landing the pitch or being turned down. If you need to speak to an employee, at the right time and place makes having tough conversations a lot easier. It also shows you have respect for their privacy and dignity.

Honesty Is Always the Best Policy
There is a fine line between being honest and too honest. Learn how to walk that line. While being open and keeping people apprised of what is going on is admirable, too much honesty can have the opposite effect.

It Is Not Just Your Mouth Doing the Talking
When you are addressing someone or a group of people, it is not only your voice, tone, the words, or your facial expression(s) that is conveying a message. The way you stand, fold your arms, cross your legs, and so on speaks volumes.

You need to be aware of your body language because even though your voice may be calm, your stance could be aggressive. Work on your body language and try to keep it as neutral as possible. You need to be aware of your body language because even though your voice may be calm, your stance could be aggressive. Work on your body language and try to keep it as neutral as possible. These nonverbal cues are inserted subconsciously and if you are unaware of them, they will steal the show.

Chapter 4
Effective Communication Tactics for the Workplace

Employers value excellent communication skills in their employees. Being able to communicate at all levels makes you valuable to them.

Good Communication in the Workplace

Good communication is a necessity in the workplace as it:

Boosts Employee Morale

When the lines of communication are open between the hierarchy in an organization, it leads to high morale in the workplace. Employees have more confidence in their work and their management structure, and it makes a better working environment.

If employees know they can count on you, they can talk to you, and that you are listening to them makes them feel valued. Employees who feel valued want to come to work and they attempt to ensure they produce quality work. When employee morale is high, it cuts down on speculation and workplace grapevines.

Employees like to be kept abreast of what is going on in their workplace. It also gives them more stability and job assurance.

Helps with Conflict Resolution

Uncertainty and misunderstandings in the workplace are two of the top causes of workplace conflict. Not keeping employees involved or apprised of changes or company news is another sure path to the conflict in the workplace.

Having excellent communication skills is knowing how to effectively mitigate conflict and nip it in the bud without too many ruffled feathers, as most workplace conflict boils down to some misunderstanding or other due to poor communication.

Encourages Employee Engagement

When employees know what is going on, they feel more inclined to be more involved. Getting employees more involved increases productivity as it leads to a more knowledgeable workforce.

Boost Production
Employees with high morale put in more of an effort into their work. As they feel valued by their employer, they take pride in what they do. When employees are happy in a company, they will automatically look to expand their knowledge and grow within the company. This is good for a company as it keeps experienced employees.

Leads to Better Client/Customer Relations
Happy customers are repeat customers and that keeps a company going. To have happy customers, your staff needs to know how to communicate with them. You can produce the most perfect product or flawless service, but you won't keep your client base if the employees are rude to the customers.

Effective communication helps to establish a rapport with clients or customers. In this current environment of social media, the last thing you want is an unhappy customer with thousands of followers. Large corporates can be a pain to work with at times, but you must learn to smile and be polite.

Tips and Tactics for Better Communication in the Workplace

Poor communication skills not only hinder the people you work with but you as well. They are one of the top reasons that an employee does not advance as quickly in the workplace as they should. If you are a manager or a supervisor, it is up to you to ensure your team operates to its maximum potential and uses valuable resources.

As an employee, if you can communicate effectively at all levels within the organization, you immediately become a valuable asset. Companies need people who can mitigate the obstacles in a working environment and encourage good workplace morale. The following tips and tactics are a good place to implement effective communication in the workplace:

Implement an "Open-Dooor" Policy
An open-door policy does not mean a physical door. It means that you are always there to help, listen, and guide your fellow employees or team members. If you are in charge of other managers or team leaders/supervisors, you need to make them implement this policy as well.
You need to make people feel you are approachable and there for them. This makes them feel more secure in their working environment because you have taken an interest. A major cause of employee dissatisfaction and turnover is because they feel undervalued, taken for granted, and downtrodden.

Always opt for Face-to-Face Meetings
When you are emailing, talking over a phone, or messaging words can easily be misunderstood. This is especially true across a cultural divide or even a hierarchical structure. The sad truth about emails, phones, and messaging is that people do not always read what is written correctly. They may not fully understand what has been written, and when you are talking on the phone, anything around them can be a distraction.

You may think you can talk on the phone and do something else at the same time, but you are not giving either your full attention. It is like listening with one ear or trying to see with one eye—you are missing the other half of the situation. Meeting face-to-face to discuss issues and important matters is the best way to cut through misunderstandings. It is also the best way to gage whether the person understands and agrees or disagrees with you.

In this world of technology and offices scattered all over the world, there will be times when meeting in person is not an option. But this world of technology does offer many a meeting platform that allows for face-time calls. Effective communicators have to get over being camera shy! This means that you cannot just have the camera switched on their side and not yours. Any form of communication is a two-way street and having a one-sided face-time conversation is more of an interrogation than a meeting.

Check Your Body Language
A person does not even realize what their body language is screaming to others. Attempt to relax your body and try not to fold your arms when talking or lean in when making a point. Make eye contact with the person you are speaking to to show you are listening and concentrating on the issue at hand. Not making eye contact can come across as cagey, shady, disinterested, or even disrespectful.

Educate
Always make sure others have fully grasped or understood what you are trying to say. Keep technical or corporate jargon to a minimum and rather talk in everyday terms. When you throw corporate or technical jargon into the conversation, it usually goes over most people's heads. This jargon can also have more than one meaning, so it can be confusing, and people will just switch off. It also makes them feel you are talking down to them or just expect them to know what you are talking about. Make your conversations clear and concise. Speak in terms and a language everyone can understand. This shows employees you are trying to bridge the gap and make things a lot easier for them to grasp or understand. They will respect and come to trust you more for it.

If you suspect a few employees are not grasping something, rather approach them directly and discreetly than head-on or around their peers. Then work around their level to help them understand. Make training interesting, fun, and do your homework, so employees will enjoy what training. Have engaging workshops where employees can swap their ideas and show off their skills. This ensures a working environment with a cross talent beneficial to any company. Employees value a company that values them by investing in their future. This shows you want them to move up and keep their skills in the house.

Use Your Inside Voice
Seriously, learn to calm down if you have an explosive fuse. This may even require you to go for anger management, leadership skills courses, or therapy of sorts. There is nothing worse than a person that erupts (reacts) to a situation instead of responding to it.

This creates discord within the workplace and creates more problems than it solves. Who can work in fear of antagonizing someone? It is like having a bully in the workplace, so a person tries to fade into the background for fear of being singled out. If there is a problem, people will try to fix it on their own or cover it up instead of approaching the relevant person. You need not be a genius to figure out what problems this can cause down the line. Rather walk away until you have yourself under control than verbally attack someone. That is personalizing the issue instead of focusing on the problem (this has been discussed in a previous chapter). Listen to the problem, go away and think it over, then possibly call the person into your office for a quiet chat. Go over the issue with the person and then ascertain if it is a training issue or another issue.

Practicing diplomacy goes a long way to gaining trust in the workplace. An excellent communicator instills trust in those around them. They also never use demeaning names or belittle anyone in a crisis or experiencing a problem. Always get to the root cause instead of applying band-aid fixes.

Lead by Example

Leading by example may be an old cliché, but it is a very important factor in being an impressive communicator. You may feel a little deflated or down because you have just discovered you have been the problem. Cheer up because a lot of other people around you also have a problem with communication. Your problem is probably more visible because you are more in the spotlight than they are. This is your chance to help those that slink away in the background because they have problems with communication.

By overcoming your communication and people skills problems, you are already becoming a shining example. By being able to effectively communicate at all levels, you're setting the tone in the workplace. Once others see how you have turned the tide, they will naturally follow your lead.

Where to Start Communicating Effectively at Work

Now that you know what is needed of an effective communicator in the workplace, here are some dos and don'ts to get you started.

The Dos
- Keep your communication short, to the point, and concise.
- Stay on topic and try not to drag the session out; keep it to 20 minutes or fewer.
- Wherever possible, use visual aids that are stimulating and capture the point.
- Make face-to-face communication a priority. Let your team get to know you in person, even if it means having to make use of virtual meetings.
- Be consistent in your dealings with your team or work colleagues and stick to a routine.
- Always clarify communication sent via email or messaging applications. It is very easy to misinterpret written communication.
- Make sure any written or verbal communication is useful to the person you are addressing it to. This may mean you have to separate your meetings or email groups. For instance, the IT team does not want to know about the new procedure for the production team and vice versa. Sending out information that a team cannot use or does not directly pertain to them, wastes the team's time.
- Adjust your presentations, training, or communication to the level of the group you are addressing. You do not want to talk over people's heads or make them feel uncomfortable.
- Keep lines of communication open and give your full attention to a conversation, complaint, idea, or question. Let your team know you are always there for them.
- Give praise and encouragement. Introduce incentives and team-building initiatives to keep employee morale up. Engage with employees and show an interest in what they do.
- Keep employees up to date on company news and status.
- Use a performance review to help assess an employee's progress and accomplishments.

- Be observant and stay on top of employee training to ensure that all staff has the knowledge and tools to do their job.
- Be diplomatic and respect your team. If there is an issue, deal with it discreetly and effectively.
- Introduce effective communication tools such as Slack to allow for management to engage with staff and/or staff with other staff members.

The Don'ts

- Don't bombard your team with a barrage of long emails instead of holding a quick meeting.
- Don't hold a meeting without being prepared for it or having a clear goal for the meeting.
- Don't interrupt when one of your teams is voicing their opinion or pitching an idea.
- Don't be afraid to tackle the hard topics, and when you do, do so with honesty.
- Never rely on messaging software or email as a source of communication. Not only can it be misinterpreted, but some employees may not even read it.
- Leave no one out as it makes employees feel as if they are not valued.
- Never assume that what one group of employees can grasp that another group will grasp it the same. Tailor conversations, seminars, and talks around the employee(s), not the subject.
- Don't be afraid to admit you're wrong, ask for help, or delegate.
- Don't shoot an employee's idea down.

Chapter 5
Effective Communication Tactics for Relationships

Did you ever play the broken telephone game when you were a child? Some schools use it to teach children the art of listening and communicating with each other. The children are usually put into a group or in a line. The adult will whisper something into the ear of the first child who must then pass the message on to the next one. The initial sentence usually has words in it that sound similar to other words like a bunny (funny), three (tree), and so on. The last child to get the message must repeat it out loud. By the time the message has arrived at the last child, it is usually (very) different from what it started out as. The minute the first child sent on the message; it would have been interpreted how that first child heard it.

Broken telephone shows how a simple sentence can so easily be misinterpreted.

Everyone has their version of a conversation, situation, or event. Today's junior people like to say "Shut up" when expressing shock, excitement, or even joy at something. If you shouted "Shut up" to someone of a different generation, they would take it as an offense. If you are going to be able to effectively navigate any personal relationship, you need to establish rapport with the person or group of people.

Make sure what you are conveying does not end up as a broken telephone message. In personal relationships that can be difficult to do as it also depends on the other person's emotions and how they will hear anything. Around about now you are probably thinking it was a lot easier when you considered everyone an idiot. No one said effective communication would be easy. It is a minefield you have to cunningly navigate to prevent unnecessary explosions. Or at least make sure you are not the detonator but a one-person bomb squad.

Effectively Communicating Your Way Through Relationships

Have you ever watched a smooth operator, their silver tongue weaving a web of fascination and devotion as they manipulate all those around them, breeze their way through a crowd of people? They exude confidence and know just the right thing to say to anyone who will listen. Those people have what they call the gift of the gab. They know how to interpret the cues of a person's body language. With a few well-thought-out questions, they can lead a conversation in any direction.

You need not be a smooth operator; you just need to learn these few basic tactics:

Become a Good Listener
Put another person's needs above your own and for once really listen to what they are saying. Don't interpret it to what you want it to be or how you think it may be. Listen to them, see things from their point of view. This means having to take a step back and see the situation from their side of the conversation. You know, walk a day in their shoes!
Okay, you don't have to do an entire day, but at least do it for the duration of the conversation. It will surprise you just how much a person will respond to you when you just sit and absorb what they are telling you. They have probably been trying to tell you about it for a long time. Butting in when they are having their say or trying to pour their heart out to you is not only rude, but arrogant and self-serving. You are showing the person you have total disregard for their emotions, thoughts, ideas, feelings, and so on.
You need to quiet your mind and focus on the conversation. You will get your turn to talk and when you do, you will do so well-armed with information. You won't go in one-sided and you will have kept the conversation a two-way one. People like to be heard, know they have a voice, and that you appreciate and value that.

Become a Safe Space
Excellent communicators are looked at as trustworthy and reliable people. They are someone that others can go to for a shelter in a storm. People know that they can trust them with their lives. They become a safe space where someone can turn to when they need to take a minute, need to vent, or need some advice. They turn to people like this because they feel safe doing so.

The one thing that makes a person a safe space is realizing that whatever someone tells you or asks you to keep is not yours to tell or show. What is said in confidence is for your ears only and no one else's! If the confider wanted their story known, they would tell it.

Pay Attention to Other People's Body Language
Watch for what a person is not saying when you are listening to them. Their gestures, facial expressions, eye movements, and the way they position their body can speak volumes to you. While you are noting their body language, pay attention to yours as it may feed theirs.

Make sure your entire body is portraying your openness, and it is not screaming defensive, arrogant, or shut off.

Keep a Tight Leash on Your Emotions
When someone is coming at you in a heightened emotional state, your first response is usually the fight back one. As hard as it may be, pull in your emotions. Take a few deep breaths. Center yourself even if it means slipping off to a happy place in your mind for a minute.

If you erupt emotionally in reaction to another person's emotions, you are just creating an enormous boiling pot of emotionally charged hurt. That just leads to a turmoil of misunderstanding and a relationship rift. If you go into the situation emotionally yourself, you will miss out on so many other cues.

When you can reign in your emotions enough to allow another person to vent, you can hear so much more. It is not just the barrage of words pouring out their mouth, but you can also hear what they are feeling. This, in turn, allows you to understand why they are feeling it. This brings about a whole new understanding of a situation for you.

Be Respectfully Assertive
Just because you are trying to be more understanding so you can communicate with others does not mean you have to become a pushover. You, like everyone, also have an opinion and a side of the story.

Your opinions, ideas, emotions, and thoughts also count. You need to assert these in a clear, concise, open, and definitive manner.

Only you need to learn to assert yourself while still respecting other people's feelings, ideas, emotions, and so on.

You cannot be hostile, look down or talk down to anyone, be aggressive, or overbearingly demanding. You cannot treat people like they are simpletons or morons.

You need to find a common ground that will help the other person or people relate to your point of view. Be confident of your wants, likes, and dislikes while still respecting the fact others may not feel the same about them.

Learn to take criticism or constructive feedback and know that everyone needs help. Learn how to ask for it, take a compliment graciously, and give them out more too.
Don't take the entire world on your shoulders either. There is this word that is there to be used when you cannot take anymore. This word is NO. Learn to use it more and when to use it. It is important to know your limits, so you need to trust enough to delegate.
You are also allowed to be angry, upset, hurt, or feel your feelings. Just learn how to express them more productively. You are a person with your own opinions, hopes, dreams, desires, beliefs, and ways. Be proud of these; they are yours, but you cannot force them on other people. You can only accept who they are, and they too have theirs.

Be Aware of Your Own Feelings
When a conflict, heartache, or situation arises, it can either blindside you or brew over time. Either way, people bottle up what they are feeling inside, mainly because they do not want to face what they are feeling. It is easier to lash out in anger than to give in to hurt or be honest enough to say you are hurt.

It is all well and good to become an avid listener and to know when or how to assert yourself or be a shelter in a storm. But if you do not face your feelings, troubles, stresses, and such, you are a powder keg waiting to explode. You started reading this book because you realized you were the one with the communication problem causing the surrounding chaos.

You can learn various tactics and even practice them. You may even become the communicator you want to be or are striving to be. But what good is all that if you did not face what made you such a poor communicator?

It is called emotional awareness. It is something any excellent communicator has and knows how to deal with. Because how can you be aware of other people's emotions if you are not aware of your own? Just because you may control your anger, fear, sadness, and such does not mean you understand them. It simply means you are sweeping them under the rug and not dealing with them.

You will need to build on your emotional intelligence. That is a whole other book though and you will probably need some professional help. There are many ways you can develop your emotional intelligence, but suppressed emotions usually have deeper connotations. This brings us back to a previous point: don't be afraid to ask for help of any kind.

Where to Start Communicating Effectively in a Relationship

You now have a basic picture of what good communication in a relationship should be. Here are some tips on the dos and don'ts of relationship communication.

The Dos

- Keep your cool. If you cannot take a breath, go to your merry place in your mind or walk away for a few minutes. If the other person seems really aggravated and intent on pushing, ask them to give you a minute. Needing the bathroom is always an excellent excuse to walk away. Choking and needing a glass of water is another way to show you are not walking away from the conversation, but you need a minute. Those few minutes you take to breathe, calm down, and clear your head gives the other person time to do so as well. It also builds a better communication bridge and shifts their attention. It seems sneaky, but it is a lot better than saying things in the heat of the moment that cannot be unsaid.

- Be considerate of other people's feelings. Always validate another person's feelings as they are just as important as your own. Listen with your ears and your heart, be empathetic, and show compassion. Sometimes understanding how another person is feeling can help you understand your own emotions.

- Never discount your own feelings, emotions, or thoughts. It is okay to complain and voice how you are feeling. Sweeping things aside is not addressing them or getting over them; it is merely creating a pile of problems that will collapse one day. Learn how to express them in a better way and know there is a fine line between complaining and nagging. There is also a fine line between having your say and verbal or physical abuse. You have the right to complain, but so does the other party in the relationship. If a relationship of any kind is going to work, it needs to be an equal one. There should not be overbearing dominance or psychological influencing of any kind.

- Choose your words carefully. This is a "do" that comes up in all areas of communication. Even when you need to be defensive, it is better to use non-defensive words than defensive ones. Yes, that sounds confusing, but it simply means you leave out the **"you"** statements. Instead, use **"I"** or **"we"** statements. For instance, instead of "You were the one…" try "I feel maybe we should look at this from all points of view." Including yourself in the equation makes the other party or parties feel as if you are not laying blame.

- Use the one- or two-day rule. If there is a major disagreement or something that needs sorting out, put a time frame on it. Dragging things out or rehashing them means the issue was never resolved. Leaving anything unresolved is a recipe for disaster in a relationship. After the given time frame, if the problem is not resolved, maybe the relationship needs more help in the form of a professional. Or maybe it is time to take a closer look at the relationship.

- Apologizing. No matter how much you may feel you are, you are not always right. Your actions are not always justifiable, and everyone can be selfish at times. See things from the other person's point of view. Admit when you are wrong and apologize, then make a concerted effort to consider their feelings in the future.

The Don'ts

- Sulk. Becoming sullen, withdrawing, and giving someone the silent treatment is what children who do not know any better do. It shows that you feel you have either been wronged or are only thinking about yourself if you were in the wrong. Stonewalling the other party is a form of poor communication abilities and is what can make a relationship become rocky or even break it.

- Become defensive. In an argument, or if a situation arises, you need to face the consequences of your actions. Becoming defensive moves, the situation into a messier state than it already is. Addressing the issue, taking responsibility, and owning it moves the situation into a state ready for repair.

- Never criticize. There is constructive criticism, and then there is combative criticism. There may be a time and place for constructive criticism but there is rarely, if ever, a time and place for combative criticism. Instead of using statements such as "You never think of anyone else," try "Please consider other people's feelings next time."

- Never do or say anything when angry or overly emotional. This is one of the hardest "don'ts" when it comes to relationships. It does not matter how much you love or like someone, sometimes they will get under your skin. People do stupid things. Look at you; up to this point, you have probably been driving people away with your "everyone is an idiot" attitude. Now you need to have a "think before you speak" attitude. This means "don't go in with guns blazing." Not only do you not know who will get caught up in the crosshairs, but you are not thinking rashly. **DON'T BE A HOT HEAD!**

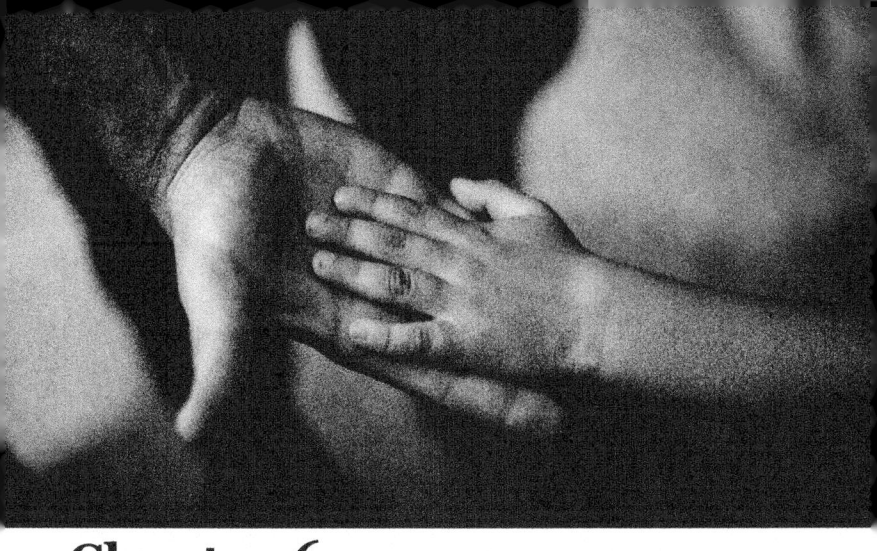

Chapter 6
The Art of Communicating with Children, Tweens, and Teens

You think being an effective communicator in the workplace or with relationships is a minefield! It is nothing compared to being able to communicate with children, tweens, and teenagers. There are guidelines on how to teach a child, how to feed them, and how to care for them but nothing teaches you how to manage each individual personality. They are not afraid of their emotions; they love expressing them, and what comes out of their mouths is the unfiltered truth.

Little people can turn your entire world upside down. They will make you wonder how you ever ran an entire work project on your own when you are left clueless about dealing with them. From the moment they give their first wail, everything you thought you knew or learned flies out the window.

If you can learn to effectively communicate with children, tweens, and teens, you are well on your way to being able to communicate with anyone. What learning to deal with and communicate with children can teach you:

Patience
One of the best tricks to dealing with children, tweens, and teens is to remember you were once one. You may think you have forgotten, but if you take a moment, you will remember how you felt in certain situations at that age.

You were once a blank slate pestering the world around you for information and not realizing how annoying you were. When you are young, all you know is that those so-called adults around you are there to help you grow and become a whole person.

To children, it is not testing the boundaries but a learning curb. Yes, they can push and push, but it is up to you as the adult to quench their thirst for that knowledge in such a way it satisfies them. They don't understand "because I say so." They want to know why you said so. If you don't tell them, they will keep on trying to find out.

You need to build up your patience to lay out a logical explanation that will appease their adolescent minds. You need to exercise this patience even more when dealing with a volatile situation that will come with dealing with tweens and teens.

Erupting or reacting to children of any age does not convey a very good message to them. It also gives them a way to push your buttons. If they can make you lose your cool, they are more likely to get you to give in, either by being so annoying and frustrating that you give in or by guilting you into getting their way.

It is difficult but dealing with children with a level head and even-tempered emotions show them they cannot get the better of you. It also shows them you are really there for them, and they can trust you. You would rather a child come to you with their problems than hide them from you.

Learning to be patient with a child changes you and helps you develop patience throughout your social or work life. Not that you need to treat everyone as a child, but it gives you a greater insight into dealing with people from all walks of life and ages.

Compassion
Children are born with natural compassion. Adults rarely realize just how much a little person feels. They may not understand it when they are young, but they feel for adults, other kids, animals, and even their toys. They can teach you a lot about caring for another human being, creature, or thing.

Once you have opened your heart to a child, it is hard to close it on the rest of the world.

Empathy
When a child cries or gets hurt, or a teenager has their first heartache, even if you are not that close to them, you cannot help but empathize with them. They live their emotions with vigor as they have yet to learn how to control them or pack them away.

It is through these pure emotions that you can learn to recognize and understand yours. If there is one thing besides endless patience, it is empathy a person needs to communicate with children. Until you can know or feel their pain or what they are going through, you will never get through to them.

Accepting
There is a lot to learn under this tactic. You have to accept that a child coming into your life will change it. It does not matter if the child is not yours. Even if they are friends' kids, your siblings' children, or your partner's kids, they will change your life.

Most people frown at the mom in a store, ignoring her child having a tantrum that makes them look like the spawn of Satan himself. In your mind, you're thinking "Control your kid." Until you experience a tantrum from hell, you do not understand what that parent is going through.

When you have to deal with children, you soon come to respect the sheer will it took for that parent not to snap. How they are gritting their teeth, hoping the storm will soon pass. While they accept that their kid will go through this, the one reason they are gritting their teeth is that other people are standing there judging their parenting skills.

But the more you deal with kids, the more you come to accept the changes that take place to and around you. Children will push boundaries, they will be curious, they will make you fume, they will change who you are forever. They can pry open even the most tightly closed heart.

How to Be There
Children, even teens and tweens, require constant attention. Not the multitasking kind of attention either. They need to be supervised, fed, have homework done, be taken here, there, and everywhere. You cannot just do it as a shadow of yourself either. To make a difference in their lives, you have to be there present in every moment.

This helps you become more focused and attentive. Because if you are not paying attention around a child, you will end up with something shoved up a nostril or worse.

If you can keep a child in check, do the school thing, and run a house, you will handle just about anything at work. This includes dealing with awkward people and paying attention to the finer details.

How to Be More Considerate
Little people seem to have no consideration for anyone. They barge through their little lives unobstructed without a care in the world. But then they bring you a cup of fake tea because you looked sad. Or they give you a hug because you looked sad. It is then that you realize how considerate they can be. Also, they show their consideration with an open and pure heart.

It costs you nothing to show another person some consideration, especially the feelings, wants, and needs of a child.

How to Get in Touch with Your Emotions
Children can be rather vocal and hyperactive about expressing their emotions. They do not have the filters adults have. Their world is still innocent and open to that kind of behavior. But their feelings are genuine, and you can learn a lot about your own feelings by helping a child deal with theirs.

Most suppressed emotions can date back to childhood trauma or situation. By helping a child deal with all their emotional issues, it forces you to deal with yours too, especially when you know the best way to help the child is to remember how you felt at that age.

How to Live
They may turn your life upside down and frustrate the heck out of you. But what they can do is also bring the joy back into it. They can teach you how to relax and enjoy life, especially as you get to see it through their eyes as a fascinating new place.

Where to Start Communicating Effectively with Children
You may not have kids, but at some point, you will need to deal with them. If you have kids, this section will help you deal with tips to effectively communicate with them. From the moment a child knows the cues to get their career running, they have learned the art of communication. Their brains are sponges from the moment they are born. They also never stop learning right into adulthood—look at you, learning new communication skills. You may think each age group needs to be treated differently, but that is not true. You need to set the precedent and then adjust it according to the age group.

For example, when your child is young, you pick out their clothes for them. When they move into the next age bracket, it is no longer cool for their parents to pick out their clothes. They are also developing their own personalities. Instead of becoming defensive about it, pay attention to what they like. Show an interest but be careful not to be too pushy or intrusive. As discussed before in this chapter, never forget you were once a kid too. Use your own experience to help you connect and communicate with the child. Using these tools, you can point them towards clothes you saw in a "certain store" that they may like. Now you are being understanding, not mocking their style, and giving them the freedom to choose while still maintaining some control.

Teenagers are the worst to figure out as they are going through a lot. Keep that in mind when they hate you, slam doors, or try to run away at least once a week. Dealing with teenagers is like being at the Mad Hatters Tea party. There are a lot of strange things going on and the table is filled with equally strange and confused characters. What teenagers need is what all kids need: guidance. You, like it or not, are their guide. They are looking to you as an adult for direction. If we look at the example of choosing their clothes, for a teenager, it is better to ask their advice or opinion on the best place to shop. During the conversation, you can slip in places you have noted or liked to shop at when you were a teen. Don't forget to mention how quickly fashion from the various decades always circles back. What you have done is kept the precedent but changed the presentation to suit the age group of the child/tween/teen.

Here are some tips on the dos and don'ts of communicating with children, tweens, and teens.

The Dos

- Lay down the ground rules; be firm and fair.
- Adjust and move with the times. Children grow rather fast and you must be willing to grow with them. This means keeping the ground rules but adjusting them accordingly as they mature.
- Always talk to them and not at them. When you talk to a child, it means you are invalidating their feelings, dreams, emotions, and ideas. You are putting out the message that you do not care what they think, and you are talking down to them. Talking to them means you are including their opinions into the equations and validating their feelings, emotions, and ideas. You are seeing them as little individual people that have minds to think for themselves.
- Make family time. It is very important to have family time. Even with sulky self-absorbed teenagers. As a family unit, you need to talk things out and let everyone have a go. As an adult, you need to ensure the conversation stays within the PG rating and stays level-headed. This is the time to teach children how to take five, think, and then communicate with a clear head. No, this is not a simple task, because children have no emotional filters! But as an adult, you need to lead by example and be able to keep your cool. By making family communication time, it also teaches children the art of open and honest communication. It is also a time when all electronic devices need to be put away. The one thing the new generation lacks is the art of verbal face-to-face conversation.
- Express how you feel in a calm, open, and honest way. Tell your kids you love them often. Tell them how proud you are of them. Even if they have failed at something, let them know how well you think they did. Children hate to disappoint their family, so you need to let them feel it is okay to stumble. Life is full of trials; they will get knocked about by it. They need you to be the one who lifts them up, dusts them off, puts a band-aid over their pain, makes sure it heals, and keeps their spirits up.

- Be understanding, forgiving, and firm. You don't have to become Godzilla to drive your point home. Listen to what they have to say, calmly let them know they messed up, and you hear what they have said. Then lay out the punishment that fits the crime by being fair and making sure they understand why they are being punished. Even when kids mess up, they tend to misunderstand why they are being punished.

The Don'ts

- Don't break their spirit. "It is easier to build strong children than to repair broken men" (Frederick Douglass Biography, 2020). Children come into the world as a blank canvas. They fill that canvas with splashes of color. It may not be what you like or agree with, but they are not you. They see everything differently, and no one has the right to change that. Rather guide them and steer them; don't tear them apart. Let them ride their imaginations. Answer their questions as truthfully as possible and rather say you do not know than fob them off. Then research the answer together.

- Don't play favorites. Never compare one child to another. Each is uniquely different. Never give to one child without giving to the other. Never set a standard or limit for one child and not the other. By doing so, you are playing favoritism.

- One child's mistake should not be a punishment for others. When it comes to setting rules or punishments, do not base it on what you may have done when you were a kid. Do not base it on what your parents did when you were a kid. That is not fair as times change, parenting evolves, as do children. Do not set impossible standards or punishments because of what one of your kids or a kid around them may have done. You may think you are protecting them, but you are not; you are judging them before giving them a chance.

- Don't make an example out of them. Children will mess up. They will continue to do so throughout their life. Once again, look at yourself and remind yourself why you are reading this book in the first place. Using their mistakes as an example is rubbing salt into a wound you are not letting heal. They are more likely to go right out and do whatever it is again. Only this time they will probably take pictures and send it to you as a slap in the face as you were the one who inadvertently threw down the gauntlet.

- Don't down their dreams. Children of all ages have overactive imaginations. The world to them is still full of magic and wonder. Let them live in that world for as long as they can. You can keep them grounded, but never squash their imagination or laugh at their dreams.

Chapter 7
Effective Communication Tactics for Everyday Life

Being a great communicator does not stop with work, relationships, and dealing with children. It also affects how we go through our day-to-day lives and the people we encounter along the way. People like the bus driver, shop assistant, delivery person, postman, and so on. These are the people who function on the outskirts of your life. You barely notice they are there except for a dismissive nod here or there.

Becoming an effective communicator does not stop once you step out of your front door or office. It needs to be carried through to that space between the two as well. If you go for a run, there is nothing stopping you from being courteous to other joggers. Helping a little old lady across the street and asking the shop assistant how they are costs you nothing. It does, however, make the shop assistants' day that someone noticed them. The same should apply to servers at a restaurant. Say please and thank you, let them know you were happy with their service. There is nothing wrong with common decency, which the world seems to be sorely lacking these days.

Simple gestures that make someone else's day and help you become a better communicator, if not person, include:

Smiling
Smiling can make a person feel better after a long hard day if you are angry or upset. When you are feeling emotional, it can be one of the hardest things to do. But if you do, your brain will reward you by releasing neuropeptides. These are small molecules that are helpful for fighting off stress and anxiety. Once these teeny little molecules are released, other neurotransmitters are set free into the bloodstream. These powerful hormones include the likes of endorphins, dopamine, and serotonin. They are what science refers to as "endogenous opioid neuropeptides" ("The Health Benefits of Smiling", n.d.) that make a person feel happy. They are also a natural antidepressant and pain reliever.

Like a yawn, smiling is also catchy and is the one thing no one minds catching from another person. In fact, you are passing on happiness! It also makes you look more relaxed and comfortable in your skin; you come across as confident. So, you are not only making your day a little better but someone else's too.

Everyone around you has their own story and happenings in their life. Sometimes, all it takes to make their day a little brighter is a genuine smile from a stranger. Your grocer, pharmacist, and bus driver are there to help make your life easier. Thank them with a genuine smile as they have probably taken a lot of flak from troublesome people all day.

Greeting
How hard is it to take a moment to start a conversation with hello or hi? Most people will get onto a bus without even greeting the bus driver. Some will take the same bus every day and not even realize they have the same driver. TAKE NOTE!

Greet! A smile and a "Hi, how are you today?" cost you nothing but mean the world to those serving you. It makes them feel they matter, and you value them. See where this overlaps with your working environment? You also find that when you greet and pay attention to tellers, busboys, and servers, you may even get preferential treatment.

The world may have become closer, but people have never been further apart. No one takes notice of what is going on around them anymore; they are too busy looking down. Effective communicators know they need to keep looking ahead and around them. If you cannot take notice of your surroundings in your day-to-day, what are you missing in your home or office?

Being Polite
You can be angry and polite at the same time. For instance, if someone backs into your car, your first instinct is to get out and call them all sorts of names. That is what they are expecting. So, by the time they have climbed out of their car, they have either filled their head with excuses or are all fired up and ready for a fight.

What they are not expecting is for you to ask them if they are all right. Right there you have already gained the upper hand and deflated their counterattack or excuses. You have also redirected the conversation to make them think about if they have been hurt.

You have been polite and shown a bit of compassion. You have diffused any aggression and now you can ask what happened and for their credentials.

Use your manners and remember to say please and thank you. What always floors a cashier is when you flash them a smile, thank them, and tell them you hope they have an enjoyable day further. You are the customer that will stand out as polite and caring. You are the customer they will remember in a good way and not the one that treated them like nothing or an idiot.

Being Courteous
You may have had a long hard day but if a pregnant woman, handicapped, hurt, or elderly person needs a seat, offer yours to them. They may not take it or be a grumpy soul, but at least you have tried. If they take it, it is an awesome feeling being a hero for a minute or two.

Lend a helping hand when you see one is needed. Like picking up runaway oranges from someone's broken shopping bag. Helping a short person get something off the top shelf and asking someone if they are okay if you see something is wrong.

Start Effectively Communicating in Everyday Life
Now that you have an idea on how to navigate communication in your work life, relationships, and dealing with kids, it is time to look at the in-between. This is the communication you have with the grocer, server, that jogger running past you, the bus driver, or the person you stop at a red light next to. They are strangers that pass you or interact with you when you move from your personal life into the world as discussed in this chapter. It is important to practice excellent communication skills throughout all aspects of your life. You can't be a saint to some and an idiot to others; that shows you are not fully committed to not being an idiot.

The Dos

- Smile and nod if you catch someone's eye. Attempt to smile at the person serving you at a restaurant or store. It will make both of you feel better, and don't worry if they do not smile back. At least you know you were not the idiot this time.

- Offer to help someone if they are struggling. For example, help that little old lady across the street while making light-hearted conversation that does not make her feel like a burden. Be polite to the traffic; you may have to stop to get safely across the street even if they honk and scream at you. Once again, you know you are not the one being the idiot.

- Mind your p's and q's even if the other person is rude and obnoxious. Shake it off as once again you know you are not the one being the idiot with poor communication skills.

- Always respond to the small talk those that are serving you may offer and return questions. For example, if they ask you how you are doing today, return the question once you have answered. Then leave them with a statement of something like "Enjoy the rest of your day" or "I hope you day gets better."

The Don'ts

- Don't change your attitude because someone did not smile back or return your greeting. People are weary of other people or need to read this book as well because they are the problem in their lives.

- Don't be pushy or feel hurt if someone refuses your offer of help. Smile and back off politely. You tried and did your good deed. It is up to them to accept your help or not.

- Don't take someone else's poor mood personally. You do not know what is going on in their lives. If they are rude, just step aside and let it go. It is not your problem; don't make it so by being defensive or aggressive.

- Don't be quick to judge others. If you don't know them, don't judge them by their appearance or attitude.
- **<u>Never talk down to anyone</u>**. Keep things light when you are addressing anyone.

Chapter 8
Characteristics of an Effective Communicator

There is a lot to consider when learning how to be a more effective communicator. Get your head into the correct mindset to change years of ingrained communication habits. Although you should never compare yourself to others, what you can do is gage your progress on whether you display the following characteristics and how well you portray them.

Characteristics of a great communicator include:

Full Attention Listening
How many times has this point been covered throughout this book? That is because it may be the most important characteristic of an excellent communicator. No matter how good you think you are at multitasking, when it comes to listening, you are not!

You may think you can walk and talk on your phone at the same time, but you are still not giving the conversation your full attention. If you are giving it your full attention while walking, driving, or doing something else, then you are not concentrating on that something else.

There are some things you can quickly multitask through while having a conversation. It is still rude and half-hearted but doable. But having to make decisions, get status updates, or for something important, you need to stop, step aside, pull over, or take a moment to give the conversation your full attention.

A conversation needs to be fully absorbed for you to be able to reply accordingly. If you are rushing or doing something else while you are having a conversation, you are not taking in the entire conversation. You can miss out on important bits and, as such, are more likely to misinterpret or forget parts of the conversation. That is because your brain is receiving a lot of other visual cues while you are talking.

If you are concentrating on the conversation, your mind fixes in on its surroundings. That is why when you recall a conversation, you can remember standing in front of Starbucks, or the color yellow, etc. It is easier to recall the conversation and what was said because your brain was not busy processing other visual cues at the time.

If you are having a one-on-one with a person, they appreciate your full attention. It shows you are genuinely interested in what they have to say. It shows your commitment to helping them or wanting to partake in the conversation and you are 100% present in it.

No Distraction Focus
One secret to be an excellent communicator is having a razor-sharp focus. To do this, you must cut out all distractions when you know something requires your full attention. If you think about it, you will realize just how annoyed you get when you are in a discussion and someone answers their phone. That is so rude and scatterbrained of a person, right?

Now, if you think back a little, you will realize just how many times you have done that to someone. The first characteristic of an excellent communicator is to listen with both ears and brain in gear. You may stop the conversation or discussion to take the call or message, but you have also interrupted the conversation flow. In a chapter above, under being polite, an example was used on how to throw a person off their train of thought. When you get distracted by a phone call or some other interruption during a discussion or conversation, it is the same thing.

You lose the moment and the thread of the conversation will never be the same, particularly because the one who was interrupted will be feeling a little angry and irritated. They have good cause to be, and if you are honest with yourself, you know how you would react if the tables were turned.

Excellent communicators know how to plan and put such contingency plans into action. They also know how to politely and respectfully navigate the situation if an emergency that requires their attention arises.

An effective communicator turns down or turns off their phone in a meeting, during a conversation, or discussion. They limit as many outside influences or distractions as possible when they know the discussion is important.

Relates to Others
When you have learned to tune out distractions and listen intently to others, you will find you are better able to relate to them. To be able to speak another person's language, you need to understand them. Once you can relate to them and show you understand who they are, their situation, and what they need, you form a rapport with them.

If you do not want what you have to say to fall on deaf ears, you need to capture your audience's attention and keep it. To get your message across, you need to know you are conveying it correctly. You do not want to talk about a pork sandwich you had that morning to a group of vegans or vegetarians. Instead, you want to discuss the value of plant-based diets and good hydration.

Even if a topic or subject is not your cup of tea or belief, remember it is the other person's. So, respect that and look at it from their point of view as you will be able to better address and discuss the situation. It also ensures the other party or parties clearly understand what is being discussed.

Clear and Concise Conversationalists
Good communicators know how to translate the complex into a more simple and easier understood form. This ensures the content is engaging, captivating, and gets through to the target audience. To be an excellent communicator, you need to be able to rephrase the narrative so it can be understood on all levels.

Confident
Excellent communicators talk up and make sure they can be heard. They use the tone and pitch in their voice to their advantage when getting a point across. They exude confidence in the topic, the way they carry themselves, and the way they let their body language enhance their speech.

They speak with clear tones, pronouncing their words, and making sure their voices are not raised or too soft but resonate with their audience. They are loud and clear with what they are discussing and do not hide behind nuances and vague suggestions.

They come across as an expert in the topic at hand and have the information to back them up.

Stay on Topic

There is nothing worse than trying to have a conversation or wanting to hear a speech on a topic to have the speaker floundering and going off-topic. Excellent communicators stay on topic, ask specific targeted questions, and offer details on the subject. They know how to handle those trying to steer the topic in another direction or trip them up. That is because they are well prepared, can think on their feet, and know how to diffuse any situation.

Speak up When Necessary

Effective communicators do not butt in or interrupt a conversation to inject their two cents worth. They know when to speak up or to leave well enough alone. They can spot when someone needs help or not and have enough tact to practice diplomacy if need be.

Always Open for Discussion

An effective communicator makes them available and approachable. They are there to help and they will never leave a person hanging with a half-baked answer or leave them confused. They make sure everyone has their say, knows what is going on, and fully understands the topic. They leave no room for error and make sure that anyone who needs to clarify anything knows they can always ask.

Excellent communicators never leave the other person feeling like they are an idiot. This leaves them feeling like they can come back as many times as needed.

Not Afraid to Ask

As open as they are to receiving questions, they are just as open to asking them. To provide valid and informative information to their audience, they will ask them questions. This ensures they fully grasp the situation and leave no room for assumptions that can lead to misunderstandings or confusion.

Interpret Non-Verbal Cues

The last characteristic on this list is non-verbal cues. Effective communicators are able to interpret the other party or parties' body language. By watching how the target audience responds by their body language helps the communicator better gage their audience. Watching how a person sits, their eye contact, facial expression, or movements tells the communicator how to adjust their message to engage that person.

Body Language

When you were a child, you were probably quick to pick up on your parents' or guardian's body language, especially when you knew they were not happy, or you were in trouble. A person can talk as calmly and cool as possible, but their posture can belie their words, just like a tone of voice can change a simple statement into an aggressive one.

Understanding a person's body language gives you the edge in a situation. You can pick up on the undertones or what they are really feeling. When you understand body language, it helps you become more aware of your own non-verbal communication.

To be an excellent communicator, you need to be able to communicate effectively both verbally and non-verbally. You need to know how to adjust or keep your body language engaging and open.

Negative Body Language

- Folded arms across the body show disinterest, distrust, anger, or a defensive attitude. It can also show that someone is unsure or shy depending on the situation.

- Looking down and not keeping eye contact shows uncertainty or that a person is trying to dodge being singled out. If their arms are folded and they are looking down, they will not engage.

- If their body is turned away from you, no matter how slightly, they are not engaging with you. Or they feel uncomfortable with you, so proceed with caution, especially if they will not maintain eye contact.

- Blank, tense, or slightly squinted eyes shows the person has no trust in what you are saying. They may even challenge you.

- Touching their face, scratching their head, or fiddling with their nose is cagey means they may be dishonest or trying to hide something.

- Hands on the hips show they are not open for discussion. It can be construed as an aggressive or dominant stance.

Disinterested or Disengaged Body Language

- Scribbling, doodling, or writing arbitrary notes means the person is not paying full attention. They are disengaged, bored, or disinterested.

- Slouched or slumped posture shows the person is completely bored and not paying attention to what is going on.

- Fidgeting, fiddling, or picking at clothes shows they are tired of the subject. Although they seem to pay attention, they are not and are shutting down. The actions they are doing are to try to keep them focused.

- Staring off into space means that you have lost them. They are no longer in on the conversation and off somewhere else in their mind. Or they are trying to find something more interesting to focus on.

- Head resting in hands shows boredom, disinterest, and want for the whole thing to be over as soon as possible.

Positive Body Language

- Arms relaxed at the side of the body show you are open for conversation.

- Standing with a relaxed but upright posture shows confidence but not arrogance or aggression.

- Arms resting comfortably on armrests or not folded makes you more approachable.
- Keeping eye contact means you have nothing to hide and are open and honest.
- Soft, relaxed, and open facial expressions show you are comfortable in your own skin. It comes across as not being judgmental, kind, and open.

Projecting Body Language Tips

- If you are going to shake hands, make sure it is a firm handshake. A handshake that is too soft appears weak and submissive. One that is too firm can appear rude and aggressive or dominating.
- Stand up straight but relaxed with an air of being comfortable in your own skin. This shows you are confident and sure of yourself but not cocky or egotistical. Do not put your hands on your hips as it makes you come across as overbearing or dominating. Crossing your arms or ankles can make you seem defensive and untrusting. You can also come across as unsure of yourself, timid, or shy.
- Do not touch your face, twirl your hair, scratch the back of your neck, or rub your forehead. This is seen as a sign of frustration, irritations, or that you are not being open and honest.
- Keep your head up, especially if you are speaking in public. Keep your posture centered to show you are completely in balance. Leaning, either way, can come across as arrogant or like you are trying to hide something.
- Try not to use too many hand gestures when speaking. This can distract the audience from what you are saying. Use open hand gestures that are pointed towards the audience, showing engagement.

- Keep your body facing your audience. Turning slightly to the left or right shows you are not completely in the moment.
- Maintain eye contact and do not dart your attention all over the place. Stay focused on the audience in front of you.
- If you feel you are losing your audience, lean in towards them. This makes them feel you are about to tell them a secret, so their attention will once again be focused on you.
- In a meeting, to build a rapport with the speaker or person you are addressing, subtly mimic their posture. Do not completely mirror it; you are not trying to be a mime! You are simply putting them at ease using their body language cues.
- Use hand gestures, facial expressions, and posture to show your interest in the topic.

If you feel you cannot interpret a person's body language, use selective questions to gage their reactions. Engage the person on a topic and watch how they respond to certain questions or opinions. This can help you sort out mixed signals or hard to define body language.

Chapter 9
Building Effective Communication Bridges

Being an effective communicator means knowing how to build effective communication bridges. No, this has nothing to do with technology; well, at least not in the way of an IT bridge. It is being able to take a conversation and move it in the direction you want it to go no matter how it started out.

Being able to create a communication bridge helps to stop the communicator from getting trapped into a conversation or situation they do not want to be in. This comes especially handy for interviews, interrogations, or Q and A sessions. You will be able to produce the outcome or information you want to convey.

For example, the scenario that was discussed in an earlier chapter where someone backs into your car. By asking them how they are, you created a communication bridge to steer the conversation to where you wanted it to go. It would also be a way to diffuse any awkwardness or aggression.

Clever ways to build a communication bridge include:

Taking Charge of the Narrative
Ask the first question. For instance, if your spouse is mad about you spending money on something and comes to confront you, ask them what that item they asked you about the other day was because you were looking into the best place to buy it. Here, you are offering them something to balance out what you bought. You are also diffusing the blow up by showing them you were paying attention to their hints.

Don't get sucked into questions you do not want to answer or feel you can't in any area of your life. If you are pushed that way, don't be afraid to show you are not too sure of that topic, then move them on to the topic you want to talk about. For example; "I would love to answer that, but I am not too sure about it; however, ..."

Ask and Answer Your Own Question
You can move a tough topic into one that is more comfortable for you by answering with a question which you answer. For example:

"Do you know the reason few people talk about that topic?"

"Well, I will tell you; it is because they find this topic to be the answer..."

Keep Quiet and Contemplate

Rather than pander to a topic, conversation, or question you are not comfortable with, stop talking. Sit back and use your body language to steer the conversation in another direction. Silence can speak volumes. Look like you are contemplating what the person said and if you want them to change the subject, make them squirm a little.

Create an Amicable Atmosphere

Try to keep the atmosphere comfortable and open. It should always seem as if there is a two-way bridge for the communication path. You may steer the conversation to your side, but you will have to allow the other party a bit of communication control. It is all about being subtle, open, and not completely controlling the conversation. You need to appear to be cooperative. Watch for body language signs and know when to give a little to keep your communication bridge open.

Use Your Verbal and Non-Verbal Words

Keep your body language relaxed and open. You are trying to build up people's trust in you. Always be conscious of your vocal pitch while speaking and try not to get too excitable. Keep on a calm and even level that mimics your confident, relaxed posture.

Choose your words wisely and remember to think before you speak, even if this means taking a moment to contemplate. Use a whimsical smile or look like you are giving it some thought to keep the other party engaged. If you are unsure of the topic, use one of your bridging tactics to move the conversation on to a topic you are more familiar with.

You can inject a "funny story of relevance" using your voice and body language to help you transition away from the uncomfortable topic.

The Difference Between a Talker and a Communicator
When words are coming out of your mouth, you may talk, but that does not mean you are communicating. Talking is forming a bunch of words and then expressing them verbally, hoping the other person understands the point you are trying to get across.

Talking is usually a one-sided conversation as when you start to talk, it opens up the door to a conversation. But until the other person has responded coherently or become involved in that conversation, you have not really communicated with them.

Communicating involves being able to successfully have your message delivered, received, and understood by the recipient of the communication. It involves developing the skills to effectively communicate the message and the ability to effectively receive the feedback.

A superb example of talking versus communicating would be in a country where you do not speak the language. You can ask the person for direction in your own language, but to them, they are just hearing foreign words that make little sense or mean nothing to them. You might learn to speak the language, but even then you may not get the meaning of what you want across to them. A communicator would learn the culture, watch the person's body language, pick up on visual cues, and find a way to get their point across. Communicating means being able to improvise where necessary and using your body language, expressions, and even visual aids to make a point.

If you are giving a presentation and you stand up on the podium talking in one tone as you drone on, you will lose your audience. That becomes just you standing up there droning on about whatever it is you are droning on about. You can almost bet that after the presentation there will not be a lot, if any, people who took in a word you said.

If you are giving a presentation and use visual aids, put animation into your voice and engage the audience, and you will get a completely different outcome. You do not have to be a genius to move a crowd on a subject. But you must be well prepared, know your audience, and then appeal to them to be an effective communicator and not just a talker.

Simple Exercises to Practice Effective Communication
There are a few games you can play to help increase the ability to actively listen and communicate.

You will need a group of four to eight people, excluding yourself. You are there to manage the teams and learn to pick up on non-verbal cues. You will also get to know each person on a level you had not noticed before.

What Is the Emotion?
This is a game that can be awkward at first, especially if you are doing a work team-building exercise. No one likes to express their emotions as it makes them feel vulnerable and raw. What the game accomplishes is teaching the participants to practice empathy. It also teaches them to identify the signs when a person is struggling and helps each person to understand the other better.

- You will need to create a few cards that have different emotions written on the face of them.

- You will need a timer.

- You will need to divide the group into teams of two equal participants.

- Shuffle up the emotion cards and place them face down in the middle of the two teams.

- This game is like playing charades where each member of each team will get a turn to pick a card.

- The timer will start.

- They cannot show the card to their team members but will have to act the emotion out without words.

- They will only get a minute to do so and their team members need to pick out the emotion.

- Every correctly guessed emotion gives them 5 points.

- If they cannot guess it, the other team will get a turn to guess the emotion.
- If the opposing team guesses the emotion, the original team will lose 3 points, which will be added to the opposing team's points.
- Once the card has been played through, it is the next team's turn to pick a card.
- Each team member needs to have a turn to pick a card and act it out.
- You can let the game go on for as long as you feel necessary, but most players don't like to play for longer than an hour.

Broken Telephone

The broken telephone game has already been referenced in the book under relationships. This is an excellent game to play to increase teamwork and active listening skills. It will show how each person interprets what they read and how well they communicate that information across to the other person.

- You will need to create a few cards that have different sentences written on the face of them.

- You will need to divide the group into teams of two or more equal participants depending on the number of people taking part. You need a minimum of 6 people to play.

- Shuffle the sentence cards and place them face down in the middle of the teams.

- Each member of each team will get a turn to pick a card.

- They cannot show the card to their team members but will silently read the card.

- They will then whisper what they read to the team member sitting next to them.

- That team member will whisper it to the next one until it reaches the last member of the team.

- The last member of the team needs to say out loud what they were told.

- The person who started the conversation needs to read out what was on the card.

- Every correct sentence gets 5 points.

- Once the card has been played through, it is the next team's turn to pick a card.

- Each team member needs to have a turn to pick a card and whisper it along.

- You can let the game go on for as long as you feel necessary, but most players don't like to play for longer than an hour.

Chapter 10
Sarcasm and Passive-Aggressiveness

Communicating is being able to get your point across clearly and concisely. It also means doing so without leaving debris and mixed emotions in the process. Using tools like sarcasm or passive-aggression should never be used as the principal focus. In fact, they should not be used at all, if possible. But sometimes it is acceptable to use them. That is why it is important to know how to use both tools without harming anyone.

Sarcasm
According to an article in *Scientific America*, sarcasm can boost creativity (Gino, 2015). When used in the right context and with care, they have found it to spark a creative flair! Oscar Wilde, known for his wit, once said: "Sarcasm is the lowest form of wit but the highest form of intelligence." The meaning of the statement shows that while sarcasm can hit a person hard, it also takes an intelligent mind to correctly express it. It also takes an intelligent and open mind to fully understand or decipher it.

While sarcasm can be used as a weapon to cut a person to the bone or explode a situation, it can also diffuse one or make a person think. It is how they deliver the sarcasm that can change its meaning. If your tone is wrong or even your body language, it can change the entire context of the statement.

Unless you are an expert writer, it should not be used in emails or messaging apps. It is almost guaranteed to express the wrong message when written. Even a simple comment such as "Your eggs really are not all in the same basket" can come across as offensive. You may think you are telling the person they are having a tough time or it. They may think you are telling them the situation is their fault because they are not focused enough.

At times, and depending on the situation, a sarcastic comment can break the ice. But it should never be directed at a single target or used with an intent to belittle, hurt, or humiliate anyone. It is always better to direct sarcasm at an object or generalize it. But before you throw it into any situation, make sure you know your audience and it is appropriate. You do not want to offend anyone.

In the same article by *Scientific American*, as referenced above, their research showed that people respond more positively to sarcasm from someone they knew and trusted. It also showed that because a person had to think about the comment, it opened their brain up the creative path in their brain.

The negative side of sarcasm can damage any relationship. It also makes the person dishing it out come across as an idiot who has a blatant disregard for others' feelings. According to an article in Psychology Today, "sarcasm is hostility disguised as humor" (Lazarus, 2012). You can see why it can be construed as hostility when you come to realize that the word sarcasm comes for the Greek word "sarkazein." Sarkazein translates as "to strip off the flesh" (*Sarcasm*, n.d.).

When you use sarcasm, always make sure that if your conversation were to be talked about, your comment was not preceded by "cutting" or "hurtful." Sarcasm can leave the intended target wounded, both mentally and emotionally. That is using humor to destroy another person's confidence and humiliate them. Before you use sarcastic comments, always make sure of how you would feel if they were directed at you.

Passive-Aggression
Like sarcasm, passive-aggression has a negative side and a lighter side. Passive-aggression is rebellion or retaliation that is sugar-coated by non-aggressive behavior. For instance, someone handed you this book. They may have said, "Here, read this if you dare. It may change your life." What they were really saying was "I am sick to death and tired of your behavior. Read this book and put it into practice or hit the highway!"
In that scenario, the person was being an effective communicator by not directly telling you what an idiot you are. They were also using sarcasm to challenge you into reading the book and ending the statement with a warning. That is passive aggression dished out to help someone.
An ineffective communicator would not have been that subtle in the passive-aggression towards your idiotic attitude. They would act out by avoiding meetings with you or dragging their heels on an assignment or project. Sometimes, a person could also try to

constantly undermine you and throw spanners in the works to ensure you failed in a mission, task, or project. Some passive-aggressive behavior will have a person blatantly defying any authority you may try and exert over them. They may not do it openly, but in other non-confrontational ways.

Recognizing Passive-Aggressive Behavior
Being able to spot passive-aggressive behavior in others will help you recognize those traits in yourself.

Some characteristics of passive-aggression include:

- They can become sullen or withdrawn. Passive-aggressive people will often go off on their own, withdraw, or sulk.
- They can become overly critical of others or a situation. Passive-aggression can present itself in a form of the person being overly critical of everything or everyone.
- They can be very stubborn as they dig their heels in and refuse to budge or change their mind.
- They love to lay the blame on others and refuse to take responsibility.
- They will resent you and love to rub it in that they are not appreciated or too many demands are heaped on them.
- They can be quite hostile and cynical in an underhanded way where they are not directly aggressive or confrontational.
- They can be aloof, irritable, disagreeable, and love to procrastinate.
- One of their favorite passive-aggressive games is to be purposefully forgetful.
- They can be quite bitter and cynical, and they usually have a pessimistic outlook.

What Prompts Passive-Aggressive Behavior?
It is believed that passive-aggressive behavior can be caused by a person's living environment as well as underlying health issues (Whitson, 2014).

Some underlying issues that cause passive-aggression may include:

- An overly strict upbringing.
- An upbringing where emotion or affection was not often shown.
- A traumatic experience in their life. People suffering from post-traumatic stress disorder (PTSD) can exhibit passive-aggressive behavior.
- Not trusting an authority figure, a situation, or person. This causes them to rebel in a way they are not being directly confrontational by acting out and inciting others to do so too.
- They could suffer from ADHD (attention deficit hyperactivity disorder).
- Conduct disorder whereby the person will participate in activities such as shoplifting, vandalism, truancy, and a blatant disregard for rules.
- Substance abuse.
- Stress and anxiety. When a person is put under a lot of pressure to perform, they can start to act out in a passive-aggressive way. They will say they are fine, but they are not; they are simmer near the edge of a breakdown.
- Underlying anger, frustration, not being able to express emotions, and bottling things up.

Dealing with Passive-Aggressive Behavior

If you have recognized some signs in your own behavior or that of a person or people around you, there are ways to effectively deal with the behavior.

- Therapy. If passive-aggressive behavior becomes destructive or consuming, professional help should be sought. Professional advice is the best route to take for any signs an individual may exhibit passive-aggressive behavior. This will rule out or identify any mental or physical health issue(s) the person may have.
- Assertiveness training. This training is helpful for anyone who has to deal with passive-aggressive behavior. If there

is a lot of underlying frustration, anger, and resentment, this training can help you or the person deal with these emotions. It will help to get them under control and express them in a more productive way.
- Encouraging the person to be more truthful or up front with their feelings. Do not hide behind sarcasm or smoke screens to get your point across. They need to be more direct and learn to speak up. They need to learn to express themselves in a healthier way instead of acting out.
- They should learn techniques to calm themselves down and think clearly before acting out.
- They need to learn that not everything is an affront to them and learn to take constructive criticism.
- Most of all, people who are passive-aggressive need to become more aware of their behavior and learn to take responsibility for it. These actions need to have consequences.

Dealing with a person who is passive-aggressive is very challenging. A lot of the time these behavioral patterns have been set in motion from childhood and are deeply ingrained in their character. If you can relate to these situations, you really do need to get professional help.

Being an effective communicator means knowing when to ask for help, be it work related, relationship related, or health related. Putting in all the time and effort to gain better communication skills will be thwarted if you hit this kind of stumbling block. Part of being able to communicate with people means being able to connect with them. When you are carrying around any underlying issue such as anger, frustration, or resentment it is pretty hard to connect with anyone.

Conclusion

So, you have made it to the conclusion—well done!
This could mean one of two things for you:

1. You skimmed over the chapters, not taking anything in because you are still in denial. If this is the case, then you should consider trying harder, because following the advice in this book can change your life for the better.

2. You read through the book and have taken the advice you have found in it to put into practice in your everyday life. If this is the case, congratulations! If you have not already, you will soon find your world changing for the better. Yes, there are real-life idiots out there, but isn't it nice to know there are decent people too? These decent people now include you!

There is option three, which is: you have read the book but have not yet put any of the tactics into practice. Do not sit around and wait for chances to implement these tactics; seek opportunities to do so.

Changing your living environment, diet, or daily routine is hard. Your entire world gets turned upside down, and you find you have to retrain your subconscious mind. It throws your autopilot out of whack and takes some getting used to like a fresh pair of shoes.

Changing the way you react to other people is changing a part of who you are or have become. It is not just a simple case of reprogramming your autopilot to reach for water instead of a Coke. The way people communicate gets built up over a lifetime in reaction to how they have been communicated with. It goes a lot deeper than their external comfort zones as it reaches into their psyche.

If you are moving forward, forgive yourself a few slips. Be gentle with yourself and keep moving the way you communicate with others in the right direction. Soon, you will communicate like you were born with a silver tongue.

While on the subject of being gentle with yourself, here are a few tips:

- You should also pay close attention to your energy level; some people are exhausting and may take energy from you. You can distance yourself from these people and give them the link on Amazon to this book.
- Some people instill energy, and these are the people you need in your life.
- Always listen to your gut instinct; maybe the career you have is not the one that feeds your soul. If this is the case, I highly recommend you look at a change of career that suits your needs. Life happens, and success is measured by how you respond to it. You can either wake up every day to a life that you dislike, or you can take matters into your own hands and choose what best suits you.

When you learn how to become a more effective communicator, you will learn how to take a step back and be able to pinpoint another person's behavior. What you will find when you can do this is just how much you yourself displayed all those traits. With your new-learned communication skills, you should now know the difference between talking and communicating. Although there is a time and place for them, you will judge when passive-aggression or sarcasm are the tools to use. You will also be able to distinguish between the actual idiots and those that are not.

Being able to communicate in any area of your life without your blinkers on will help you see the little things you were missing before. You will notice that people will be more drawn to you and you will have a better home and work life. If you practice effective communication in between home and work life, you will notice a lot of stress and anxiety lifting off your shoulders. You will notice that you are better received in restaurants and will get more smiles from tellers. You may even find that the bus driver will not deliberately drive off in hopes you miss the bus. He may even give you a few extra minutes to make it to the bus by waiting for you.

If you think about why you started reading this book in the first place, you will know how you felt thinking you were dealing with idiots all around you. Now imagine how everyone in your life felt about you! You will not become a master communicator overnight; it will take some time. Changing a few simple ways in which you talk to people with your expressions, body language, and vocal pitches will go a long way to getting you there.

At the end of the day, you now have the tools to change the way you communicate with others. You can take these methods and tactics with you on your journey through life or not; it is your choice. One simple change in the way you communicate can show an enormous difference in the way you come across and that is to think before you speak or act. Those few seconds mean the difference between being a great communicator and an idiot!

References

Alexis Fotos. (n.d.). *Sarcasm* [Photograph]. https://pixabay.com/photos/sarcasm-word-letters-sarcastic-2015186/

Altmann, G. (n.d.). *HandBall Faces* [Photograph]. https://pixabay.com/illustrations/hand-ball-faces-world-population-1592415/

Altmann, G. (n.d.). *Listen To Me* [Photograph]. https://pixabay.com/illustrations/note-write-with-comic-person-man-477450/

Altmann, G. (n.d.). *Motivation, Success, Thumb, Successful* [Photograph]. https://pixabay.com/illustrations/motivation-success-thumb-successful-721821/

Are You a Poor Communicator? How to Improve: Stop the damage and improve relationships. (2012, May 05). Psychology Today, https://www.psychologytoday.com/gb/blog/communication-success/201205/are-you-poor-communicator-how-improve

Axelrod, J. (2019, November 20). *The 5 Stages of Grief & Loss*. Psych Central. https://psychcentral.com/lib/the-5-stages-of-loss-and-grief/

Bosworth, P. (n.d.). *The Power of Good Communication in the Workplace*. Leadership Choice. https://leadershipchoice.com/power-good-communication-workplace/

Chinese Whispers. (n.d.). Retrieved on May 21, 2020. https://en.wikipedia.org/wiki/Chinese_whispers

Frederick Douglas Biography. (2020, Jan 13). Biography. https://www.biography.com/activist/frederick-douglass

Gino, F. (2015, November 17). *The Surprising Benefits of Sarcasm*. Scientific American. https://www.scientificamerican.com/article/the-surprising-benefits-of-sarcasm/

Hain, J. (n.d.). *Hands Reaching Offering Child* [Photograph]. https://pixabay.com/illustrations/hands-reaching-offering-child-1022028/

Hain, J. (n.d.-b). Handshake [Photograph]. https://pixabay.com/illustrations/handshake-regard-cooperate-connect-2009195/

Hancock, J. (2009, May 17). *1983 I'm Surrounded By Idiots Pin* [Photograph]. https://www.flickr.com/photos/jdhancock/3540861791

Hassan, M. (n.d.). *Angry Business Woman* [Photograph]. https://pixabay.com/illustrations/angry-businesswoman-conflict-3233158/

Hassan, M. (n.d.). *Office Welcoming Door* [Photograph]. https://pixabay.com/illustrations/welcome-welcoming-door-office-open-3182972/

How Can We Communicate Better? (n.d.). Love Is Respect. https://www.loveisrespect.org/healthy-relationships/communicate-better/

Lazarus, C. (2012, June 26). *Think Sarcasm is Funny? Think Again.* Psychology Today. https://www.psychologytoday.com/gb/blog/think-well/201206/think-sarcasm-is-funny-think-again

Martinuzzi, B. (n.d.). *Leadership Skills: 4 Traits Of The Worst Communicators.* American Express. https://www.americanexpress.com/en-us/business/trends-and-insights/articles/leadership-skills-4-traits-of-the-worst-communicators/

Sarcasm. (n.d.). Etymonline. https://www.etymonline.com/word/sarcasm

Samson, S. (2017, July 11). *Why Do We Need Endorphins?* Healthline. https://www.healthline.com/health/endorphins

Scholfield, M. (2014, June 04). *10 Signs of a poor communicator*. BookBoon. https://bookboon.com/blog/2014/06/10-signs-poor-communicator/

Survey: Few CFOs Plan to Invest in Interpersonal Skills Development for Their Teams. (2013, June 19). Robert Half. http://rh-us.mediaroom.com/2013-06-19-Survey-Few-CFOs-Plan-to-Invest-in-Interpersonal-Skills-Development-for-Their-Teams

The Health Benefits of Smiling. (n.d.). SCL Health. https://www.sclhealth.org/blog/2019/06/the-real-health-benefits-of-smiling-and-laughing/

Whitson, S. (2014, March 16). *7 Reasons Why People Use Passive Aggressive Behavior*. Psychology Today. https://www.psychologytoday.com/gb/blog/passive-aggressive-diaries/201403/7-reasons-why-people-use-passive-aggressive-behavior

Youngson, N. (n.d.). *Communication* [Photograph]. https://picpedia.org/handwriting/c/communication.html

Printed in Great Britain
by Amazon